BOA
EDITIONS LTD

T0163877

Let's Become a Ghost Story

Let's Become a Ghost Story

poems by

Rick Bursky

American Poets Continuum Series, No. 177

BOA Editions, Ltd. ➤ Rochester, NY ⋖ 2020

For information about permission to reuse any material from this book, please contact The Permissions Company at www.permissionscompany.com or e-mail permdude@gmail.com.

Publications by BOA Editions, Ltd.—a not-for-profit corporation under section 501 (c) (3) of the United States Internal Revenue Code—are made possible with funds from a variety of sources, including public funds from the Literature Program of the National Endowment for the Arts; the New York State Council on the Arts, a state agency; and the County of Monroe, NY. Private funding sources include the Max and Marian Farash Charitable Foundation; the Mary S. Mulligan Charitable Trust; the Rochester Area Community Foundation; the Ames-Amzalak Memorial Trust in memory of Henry Ames, Semon Amzalak, and Dan Amzalak; the LGBT Fund of Greater Rochester; and contributions from many individuals nationwide. See Colophon on page 120 for special individual acknowledgments.

Cover Design: Daphne Morrissey
Cover Art: "Jolly Witch" by Marie Buckley
Interior Design and Composition: Richard Foerster
BOA Logo: Mirko

BOA Editions books are available electronically through BookShare, an online distributor offering Large-Print, Braille, Multimedia Audio Book, and Dyslexic formats, as well as through e-readers that feature text to speech capabilities.

Library of Congress Cataloging-in-Publication Data

Names: Bursky, Rick, author.
Title: Let's become a ghost story : poems / by Rick Bursky.
Description: First Edition. | Rochester, NY : BOA Editions, Ltd., 2020. |
   Series: American poets continuum series ; no. 177 | Summary: "Playful,
   sexy, and occasionally absurd, Bursky sifts through the detritus of American culture
   to reveal the sharp edges and breathtaking facets of life"— Provided by publisher.
Identifiers: LCCN 2019046061 (print) | LCCN 2019046062 (ebook) | ISBN
   9781942683995 (paperback) | ISBN 9781950774005 (epub)
Subjects: LCGFT: Poetry.
Classification: LCC PS3602.U774 L48 2020 (print) | LCC PS3602.U774
   (ebook) | DDC 811/.6—dc23
LC record available at https://lccn.loc.gov/2019046061
LC ebook record available at https://lccn.loc.gov/2019046062

BOA Editions, Ltd.
250 North Goodman Street, Suite 306
Rochester, NY 14607
www.boaeditions.org
A. Poulin, Jr., Founder (1938–1996)

for Ian Randall Wilson
—together from the beginning

Contents

THREE

FOUR

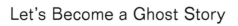

Let's Become a Ghost Story

On Some Nights I Was Her Disciple, On Others She Was Mine

She danced for tips in a bar across from an oil refinery. I drove a tow
 truck.
These were the years after the army and before college.

We shared a pay-by-week apartment. We were phobias.
We were condensation on a window waiting for a finger to write.

There was something satisfying coming home with grease on your
 hands, I told her.
As I shaved, she sat on the toilet and asked, can I pee in front of you?

Most breakfasts were a slice of toast folded over bacon or a fried egg;
 coffee, black.
You never make me laugh, she said, standing at the sink

scrubbing stains out of silk panties and bra. Nights
I practiced telling jokes while sitting alone in my truck.

She made small circles in the palm of my hand with her thumb while
 we watched television.
There was a dartboard on the bedroom wall, sometimes we played
 from bed.

I was never sure if the money she gave me to buy work boots was a
 loan.
There was something satisfying coming home with grease on your
 heart, she told me.

We were a continent of dust. The nights held us in their teeth.
Wasps and stars swarmed around us, we couldn't tell the difference.

ONE

It Doesn't Matter What the Wreckage Says

Night arrived and filled the room with fog.
She placed her hand over his eyes. This was the romance.
Then the moaning. Someone banged at a door,
that's what they thought the noise was.
Then morning soaked through the walls, everything thickened:
the shirts, the faces, pillows on the sofa,
even the house keys on the floor
that would later go missing. This was the gradual.
When I'm gone, this will be your story. Try to disown it.
Call it a hoax. Call it perjury.

Night with its cool darkness will come again.
In the morning, the fishwife will sit on a crate of lemons at the bus stop
and tell her stories that include me walking away,
shaking my head as if disappointed.
Life—practice, practice, practice—you'll never get it right.
There are other stories to be told. This is the bruise.
If I had to tell just one more it would be about
the old man, angel wings, not shoulder blades,
folded beneath his back's tired skin. The precious desecration
of my life—it's no different than yours.

Sooner or Later, Everything Comes Out

I never told you about the night
a woman took off her stockings
in an elevator and later used them to tie my hands,
or that, while waiting in a bakery early one Sunday morning,
a man's heart stopped and he fell to the floor.
This was the only time I used CPR to save a life.
I often pretended to be a doctor, it made people feel safe.
I'm anxious to tell the truth but know better; a truth
that includes if you were a fly I would regret not being a spider web.
What you don't know, this has been a test,
your responses duly recorded.
What you don't know, a single pencil
can draw a line thirty-five miles long. I have evidence
for, and against, everything.
One day we'll walk past a crowd and they'll throw kisses.
Inside every crowd is a parade,
wild shadows trailing behind.
If you were the night, I would invent
a parachute to slow your fall.

I Know Everything I Need to Know About Joy

She told me I wasn't an appropriate subject,
or I told her she wasn't; the difference
seemed important at the time but not anymore.
Summers here can burn clouds right out of the sky.
That's the backdrop to everything I'm going to say.
One more disclaimer, eventually my heart
will no longer be an excuse. I used to plan for that day,
now I know better. When we first met, she told me
her heart had a sense of humor. She also told me,
love is barbed wire, which she claimed to know from experience.
The second time I saw her was just a coincidence,
her fingers were flamboyant, I said thank you.
People can become habits. She said make a promise and I did.

The third time, I went into the bathroom and cut myself,
just a little blood, just before sex—I never told this to anyone.
This was the time in my life when I liked to spend afternoons
sleeping in empty theaters. I hoped we could improve
our relationship by pretending to be other people.
When I tongue clouds, they have the same sweet, metallic taste
I lapped up when she pressed her vulva to my mouth.
My veins were fault lines. She was an altar.
We never missed an opportunity to become small.
The last time we saw each other, we agreed
we were going to be good at being dead.
This was during the time in my life
I was practicing my ability to miracle.

There Are Things You Don't Put in a Lost and Found

I was in love with a tall, blond woman called Striker,
the president of The Naked Women's Bowling League.
Her real name was Lynnette. Every other Tuesday
at five I gave her the keys to the alley where I worked.
She dropped them in the mail slot after locking up.
One morning I found a yellow, satin bra
hanging over the soda machine.
One afternoon, a pair of white cotton panties.
I am no longer afraid of change,
so much else to fear.
Twenty-four thousand killed by lightning each year
and bowling accidents take another seventeen.

Three million people are killed by mosquitoes.
One morning a pair of stockings on the cash register.
I like to believe these were a gift from Lynnette.
When she took the keys from me
her fingers were a promise lingering in my hand.
I never told Lynnette I dreamed of us bowling naked.
I never visited her grave.
Yes, Lynnette was tragically killed.
I have Lynnette's neon bowling ball beside my bed.
I stare at it during sex. When the orgasm comes
I imagine it spinning down the alley,
the aurora borealis of a frigid night sky.

This Wasn't the First Time a Painting
of a Rhinoceros Ended a Relationship

A rhinoceros standing in a street
in front of a department store,
late afternoon just after the rain.
A passing woman has yet to close her umbrella.
A man is lighting a cigarette.
This was the sad realism that hung
over my sofa like a hard-featured sky
over the suicides' graveyard. I bought the painting
for thirty-nine dollars at a garage sale. We had sex
on the sofa, sweat and legs muddled, this is more
about chemicals and electricity,
but she kept one foot on the floor. Symbolism,
a theatrical device similar to a spotlight,
she often said things like that.
She looked over my shoulder, up at the painting,
never closed her eyes during sex.
Love is a secondhand store—she also said.

In our first apartment, we got drunk
and impaled cockroaches with toothpicks.
Think of the symbolism here. She replaced the painting
of the rhinoceros with a painting of a woman in a yellow dress
pushing a small boat into a lake. How do you respond to that?
There is nothing more cowardly than the past,
the way it constantly flees. Swans prefer to fly
at night. What do they know about darkness that we don't?
I've changed this story over the years.
The painting was nineteen dollars.
She sliced the painting with a kitchen knife.
The painting hung in our bedroom.

Details like that. What didn't change:
it was a rhinoceros, and the swans at night,
moonlight lifted on straining wings into the black.

A Theory of Evolution

In a previous life I was a cricket rubbing my legs together
in a graveyard at night. This is how I learned ecstasy.

In a previous life she was a kingbird perched on a headstone
searching the grass for insects. This is how she learned melancholy.

There was nothing left to teach each other, so we played games.
She sat cross-legged on the bed, spinning a revolver's cylinder,

when she told me she wanted to play Russian roulette.
I preferred poker, a game that favors cheaters.

In a previous life she was a frontier, I was a border town
—you know how these stories end.

One night I woke to find her rifling through my pants, draped over a
    chair.
Moonlight glowed on her bare back. I pretended to be asleep.

The day before we had agreed to steal from each other.
I couldn't decide what to take from her.

Something from the box of mistakes she hid in her closet
or her favorite color, burgundy; no, wait, that was my favorite.

As we knew we would—red-eyed and green-tongued—we left each
    other.
In a previous life she was courageous, I almost was.

She said in her next life she'll be a red mark on the side of a face
or the hand that left the mark, there are advantages to both.

In my next life, I'm going to be the strings between the puppeteer and marionette.

A woman, of course, will be the marionette, and the moon, the puppeteer.

Let's Become a Ghost Story

Let's scare each other—it's what lovers do.
We owe each other that much.
So why not, we've done worse.
Together we're under construction.
This has nothing to do with hammers and nails
any part of our bodies can be a soldering iron.
Separate we're the punchline to each other's joke.
The other night I saw a woman run naked
from a house across the street.
I wanted her to be you—fearless
warm flesh steaming, glowing in a cold mist.
You can be suffering and I can be sugar
or you can be sugar and I'll be suffering. It's up to you.
The more we collaborate the more frightening we can be.
Let's practice naked under the whitest sheets.
Let's take turns pretending to be the wind,
slip out through an open window. Let's steal things.
You steal the daffodils from the graveyard.
I'll steal the plastic rabbit from the neighbor's yard
and finally be good at something—that's the scary part.
Are you frightened yet, it's an emotion
that must be constantly relearned
like biting your tongue or mine.

Piacular

Who can sit still in the dark for the longest,
I asked. An empty room, no windows, no lights.
Shudder, but don't scream, I said, when you feel
something slide along your leg.
To make our contest more interesting
we were naked; we had been naked in the dark before.
There was that closet back in November.
Naked except for our socks,
when I pressed her past the just-hanged shirts,
her buttock ripped by a nail we forgot was there.
Her breath bloomed in my face.
Her breath, I remember, had not yet soured
even as Doctor Gorlick closed the wound
—seven braided silk sutures, the needle's
spatula-curved point pushing through, sliding out.
I remember, neither of us wanted to stop; and her breath,
I also remember, remained in back of the closet.

There Were Many Luxuries Involved

We didn't leave her penthouse for thirteen days.
Thirteen choirboys in the hallway sang
outside our door each evening. We met
when I graduated locksmith college.
She was the commencement speaker. I was the valedictorian.
She said the padlock was invented in ancient Egypt.
The key, I reminded her, was invented
three hundred years later. We were each other's tumbler,
striker plate, reminding us to take inventory before
closing our eyes at night. Every sixteen kisses
we reapplied our lipstick.
We were each other's skeleton key
—insert, turn; insert, turn.

In the locksmith world there are two competing philosophies.
The first stops entry; the second, escape.
We were each other's beautiful sadness,
the necessary latch assembly being human
requires—insert, turn; insert, turn.
We were each other's favorite story
—one was about coming; the other about standing,
back to the door to hide the hand
turning the doorknob and then pushing
past the choirboys wondering if
the stairs would be faster than the elevator.

Regarding Most of the Disheartening

We signed our love pledge in crayon.
I don't remember why, we were, after all, adults.
I'm sure it was her idea. She chose red.
When I reached for the same crayon,
she said, no. Once I woke to music,
found her playing the flute in a bathtub
full of bubbles; she only stopped to tell me
I could fuck her younger sister if I wanted.
Halfway between the beginning and never speaking,
the sobbing and laughing were interchangeable.
Before going to bed, I put on golden gloves;
she put on golden underwear.
By all accounts, our life together was mythic.
We were pieces of each other.
Our hushed voices were made of silver.
We were a poor excuse for joy,
but an excuse nonetheless.
This isn't over, she sighed,
her hushed voice a syringe.

Preparing the Proclamations

We considered the broken engines, how they choked the gears motionless
like the slowing heart sucked the movement from the man's limbs
as he stood on a ladder and painted the side of a house.
He was one of the admired—plaster in the creases of their hands,
always something, and blood, under the fingernails.

Later, we pretended he went to the mountains with the others
where all the wind that ever pushed through the world
is stacked like firewood in the back of a cave.
Before leaving, they filled their pockets with salt.

There Are Not Enough Reasons in the World

We stopped being lovers to become lion and lion tamer.
One of us knelt naked on a stool while the other pretended
something that could be confused with dominance,
an example would be the relationship shoelaces have with shoes.
Love was originally an occult concept, and it should have remained
that way—rather than require the heart to go begging.
We stopped being lovers and became a comedy duo,
honest with each other in a spotlight,
just enough laughter to mask each deep breath.
The modern idea of love as a virtue began to take shape
during the First Council of Nicaea, 325 A.D.. Other pairings we
    considered
were police partners, God/voice of God, pilot/co-pilot,
artist/model, even gave thought to night and day
but that would have made a mockery of us.
There were many things on the list but it was a long time ago and I
    forget.
We were creating our own versions of each other.
We almost became tag team wrestlers, but got tripped up
wondering if the essence of "tag team" was erotic, aspirational,
or something to be negotiated on a case-by-case basis.
Once, while lying on top of me, she began to tremble,
then shook violently and abruptly stopped,
then floated halfway to the ceiling.
She was playing God, or I was. I don't remember.

The History of Falling Is the History of Us

When she said "I love you," I told her
that my hair flew from a thousand pennants.
When I said "I love you," she told me
her mouth was a cave. We could not be any smaller,
and when we were not that, we could not be any larger.
We were a spent shell casing ejected
from the sun's chamber, an unexpected noun
uncoiling from a miraculous sentence, sometimes
we were drool sliding down the gargoyle's cracked chin.
She was pleased by all of this, I was ambivalent. Simultaneous orgasms
turned our eyes into fluorescent orbs. She was pleased by this, too.
We created rules—a who, what, where—to calm us,
and—a who, what, where—to excite us.
And always, the goodnight smell of our bodies
in the morning, a tinge of rope-burn and melted wax.

TWO

When Does the Applause Begin?

Halfway through the solo the audience realized
the cello was carved from ice.

An old woman in the front row placed her purse
beneath her seat and began to applaud.

The theater emptied into the night. The music,
a puddle drying on an empty stage, remained behind.

A man and woman holding hands ran along the street,
a newspaper above their heads; this, too, a performance.

When first discovered, ice was believed
to have more potential than fire.

In a hotel later that night, wind from an open window,
her brassiere hanging from the bathroom door.

Fortissimo, fortissimo, coda.

I'm Now Prepared for the New Exuberance

The brothers are cleaning shotguns,
sisters sharpening the edges
of polished knives. The rest of us

sit, fists clenched at our sides,
in front of televisions
as long belts of cartridges are laid

beside the machine guns.
One Christ or another is preparing
a fire in the fireplace. I swear

I didn't ask for this.
I swear that sound is a bone breaking
and all I know about anatomy is this.

The Juggernaut

A man convinces himself he is a fact,
grounding his place in the world
until the weather of years
chip away at him from the inside.
He begins to wish he were a fish
dragging water across the ocean
or a cloud pinning the sky to the ground,
labors a man could be proud of.
For three months, his mother coughs
through the night, convinces herself
she's going to die, tells him,
"I'm going to be with your father soon."
He's been dead twenty-three years.
So the man decides to become a shovel,
digs a hole so large the entire world collapses into it.
His mother calls from the other room.
He wants to believe in survival.
Isn't it enough that our lives are experiments?

I Carry a Moth in a Pillbox with Me Everywhere

Napoleon slept with spoons over his eyes
the night before he sailed from Elba.
Little is known about the night before Waterloo.
There's so much to want in this world.
This explains pockets on pants and king-sized beds.

Sleeping with spoons over my eyes was my previous
talisman, too, but talismans are like medications
—effectiveness can fade with repeated use.
Since replacing my spoons with a moth in a pillbox
I haven't had a fountain pen leak or a parking ticket.
Taking advantage of this luck while it lasts
I'm breaking desire into a schematic an architect
might hand a plumbing contractor,
changing my name to the title of a book,
and working out the mysteries
of approaching women in supermarkets.

Sometimes I think I'm a colored stone
at the bottom of an aquarium in a Chinese restaurant
and the things I think about are from the world
of captive fish. I caught my moth circling a flame.
For a long time I fed it pieces of rotten cantaloupe.
After it dies I'll replace my light bulbs with fireflies.

One Day I Won't Have to Think About This

I remember it rained and shooting stars
scarred the night after the sky cleared,
I remember those, too; and that each of us is born
with a thousand yards of barbed wire.
Those were the years my body was a freight train
for my soul and when the stars finished with the sky
they scarred my face. The barbed wire,
let's talk about the way it tears
the sky when the wind blows,
to say nothing of what it does to me.
The past is a haunted house.
The doorbells are all dead.
The love stories are put to bed.
Prayers left your knees stiff.
Would you think differently about us
if I told you I was the minotaur women stare at?
The tap tap tap you hear—
my hooves against the pavement.

The Great Broken

This began as a conspiracy. Mosquitoes gathered
on the windowsill and talked about me.
This was when people confused me
for the Himalayas, stature not size, of course,
still, when I exhaled, a snowstorm for a thousand miles.
This was when my wounds were works of art.
This was when you liked me best.

Much has changed since then.
I bought my freedom at a yard sale.
I'm no longer going to supervise your suffering.
I've discovered *The Prophecy* is a placebo and the trouble
with relationships is that they require many decisions.
Instead of putting my tongue
in your ear I decided to tell you all this.

The Great Teachers

When I was eight years old my father taught me
how to walk on water. I kept it to myself until now.
Back then there was no need to show off,
but things have changed.
The facts have darkened me.
A woman covered the inside of my mouth with graffiti,
then taught me how to tie her to a chair
(neckties not duct tape) and everything I said
became a cloud floating in one ear and out the other.

Back then our plans were nothing more than scaffolding.
It was the last Sunday in August, early morning,
the lifeguards were at breakfast
sitting in the booth beside the window
—eggs, bacon, toast, orange juice, and coffee.
Imagine my father walking behind me,
like when he taught me to ride a bike.
Imagine him reaching into the ocean as I sink.
Imagine it's too late. I might not be
everything you ever wanted, but I'm what's left.

Drama of a Sigh

The nail on my left pinkie is three and half inches long,
the length prevents my finger from burning
when I set it aflame to light an occasional cigar.
It's not attention I want sitting alone in a dark bar,
it's a small flamboyance I allow myself. I am what happens
when a meteor crashes into a forest covered in snow.
I wish I could take credit for that statement,
but a woman said it after we spent three days drinking together.
She also said when she dies she wants all the beds
she ever slept in burnt in a giant bonfire.
I kept the impracticality of desire to myself,
nodded and stared at the brown liquid in my glass,
finally breaking the awkwardness by telling her
that when I die I want every chair I ever sat in similarly destroyed.
She didn't see how that was possible. I agreed,
this was the sensibility that kept us together.
Yesterday, an ice cube in my drink took exactly six minutes to melt,
which is often thought of as a sign of good luck.
Not wanting to squander luck in a bar,
I walked out into the afternoon rain, then it hailed, then it stopped.
Sunlight between passing clouds blinked
off tall glass buildings like Morse code from God.
Before sadness was an emotion it was the eighth day of the week.
Then astronomers came along and ruined everything.

I Am a Kingdom

I flipped a coin a hundred times, came up tails only once.
So they hung me by my legs from the gun barrel on a tank,
took turns beating me with rifle butts. Blood dripped
from my ears and the old gravediggers pulled their shovels
from their throats—something learned from the sword swallowers
—and I began composing this. Before annihilation was a prayer

it was a skinny man cooking breakfast before dawn.
He cracked a yellow egg against the side of a frying pan,
poured coffee into a dirty cup from the sink.
I carried a headstone in my arms like a child.
When I died my sweat became the salt foaming on waves.
One day everything I said will be explained
by descendants of the ruthless philosophers.

I Never Knew My Father Could Play the Harmonica

I'm sitting with my mother and brother
eating chili at the small dining room table.
My father, dead twenty-six years, wears a black suit,
stands in front of the window playing the harmonica.
There's nothing original about the world,
but we get up each morning and go to work anyway.
A doctor tells us my mother's lungs have weakened.
My father is playing the blues, which I guess
he learned in prison. No one knows who's lonelier:
the ghost or the person who sees the ghost.
Not wanting to embarrass my father I don't look
at the frayed edges on his collar or the hems of his pants.
Last week I forgot to do laundry
and wore the same socks two days in a row.
My brother is first to leave the table,
says something about returning phone calls.
It's rare that we eat dinner together.
Years ago I would have said the light falling
on my father's shoulders made them look like mountains
in the distance with a moon rising behind them;
now I think cardboard theater props.
Sometimes my eyes feel like loaded guns
and I close them for the same reason guns have safeties.
I should be telling this in the past tense
but that would be the beginning of forgetting.

The Journeys

My brother cried when I told him
our older sister was killed at sea
commanding a submarine. He was six.
When she joined the navy our parents were angry,
and secretly proud. After her death
they put the photographs of her in black frames.
Years earlier, my father hijacked a truck.
My father found prison and came back years later.
My sister found the bottom of the ocean
and never returned. The past strolls
by like an old man with his hands
behind his back. I don't remember crying
when my mother told me it would be years
before I would see my father again,
but I'm sure I did. You could write the history
of a family by what's missing.
You can tell where all the photographs
once hung by unfaded rectangles of paint.

Prognosis

for William

We could be sailboats;
the truth is, we probably are.

Yesterday is the wind, our eyes,
swollen with something similar to joy;

each lie we told ourselves is a sail.
I can't name the shore we'll run aground on,

but no ocean is wild enough to sink us.
My father wore black pants and yellow shoes

on his last birthday, we walked along the pier.
Birds floated on the swells. He knew

what was coming. He said he wanted
to come back as a bird and floating

should come instinctively to people.
On the horizon, a cloud

looks like a broken chair in the sky.
You see, there are so many places to sit out there.

Perfecting the Dog Paddle

The summer before we moved to California,
my sister took me into the Atlantic,
just beyond where rolling water broke into salt spray.
It was quiet away from the people playing in the surf.
She took my hands off her shoulders.
Have you ever had water pumped from your lungs,
lying on the sand? It happens all the time,
she reminded me. I tilted my head back
to keep my mouth out of the water,
sucked enough air so I could remember
the blue sky, the sun, the details of being alive
as I sank, throat tightened, struggled, kicked my legs,
continued the panicked descent until she grabbed
my hair and pulled me, as older sisters do,
to the surface. Try again, she said, pushing me
under once more. "One day I won't be here."

The Hardness

When I was eight, my sister, sixteen,
pulled up her blouse and bra, and showed me
her breasts—petite white balloons with pink hats,
performers in an opera buffa as the curtain rises.
"You can look, but don't touch."
It was years before I realized
how perfect they were and that I had compared
every breast I'd seen since to them.
Eleven years later, I was a soldier in uniform,
a girl followed me into the men's room
at the bus station in Shreveport, Louisiana.
She wore a green shirt, jeans, short blond hair,
glasses too big for her face.
I ignored her and washed my hands.
When I turned to leave she leaned back
against the door, pulled up her blouse and bra
and showed her breasts. "For ten dollars
you can touch them." There's a hardness
to the past the future will never know.
Two days of travel wrinkled my uniform.
I wanted to ask if she had done this before.
Is it the past or future that teaches us to pray?

Ex Cathedra

What no one knows about me
is that my left ear is made of rubber.
The original was lost in an accident
when I was nineteen. As Dr. Gorlick
sewed it to the side of my head,
he said it needed to be replaced
every eleven years to appear to age
along with my face. Vanity compels me
to replace it every thirteen.
A rubber ear isn't as uncommon as you think.
One president and two movie stars had a rubber ear.
The actors appeared together in a movie
without knowing about the other's prosthesis.
Each morning I apply a lotion to the ear
so the rubber doesn't discolor. Cell by cell,
the body replaces itself every seven years.
It's simple science. I laid on my side
as Dr. Gorlick sewed. A nurse held the ear in position.
Lidocaine and something I don't remember
prevented me from feeling the blood
run down my neck and cheek.
But I could taste it and began to spit.
The nurse put gauze pads
between my lips and apologized.
Things like this happen all the time.
Someone bleeds, someone apologizes.

My Father Is Still Dead

There must be easier ways to learn things.
A darkening stretch of sky tightens my throat.
Last night strangers played bagpipes
and harps on my lawn. My father is still dead,
he never lived to be my age,
but I still want him to be my father.

This is where forever begins. In a graveyard,
I put my ear to the ground.
What I thought was music was roots
groping dark earth; through caskets, entangling bones.
Our souls are jigsaw puzzles, pieces are missing.
Everything I say leaves a bile taste in my mouth.

That Old-Fashioned Abracadabra

Everything I know about magic
I learned staring at a firing squad.
How to make an egg disappear.
Pull a ten-foot rope from an ear.
You're thinking jack of diamonds.
I'm thinking trombone, the one
I played in the marching band.
I'm thinking of how many steps are in a parade,
how many men in a firing squad.
I'm thinking about the difference
between a puff of smoke and a small cloud.
Sometimes I cut paper dolls from the newspaper.
There's magic in that, too. A coincidence
is an umbrella arriving in the mail
the day the drought ends, earthquake the day
the earthquake insurance ends.
The chandelier crashes onto the dining room table.
A finger on a trigger is a form of sex,
look it up. The crow that flies from my hat
disappears into black smoke.
It's not a coincidence that I'm still alive,
not a magic trick. Sure, it might be luck,
but I'll take what I can get.
Don't be smug. You at least could have
raised your hand when I asked
for a volunteer to fire the gun.
I have faith that I could catch
the bullet with my teeth.

The Scientist Reports on Sacrifice

The beauty of language is how
you taste each word as it's spoken.
Books, I've proved, are nothing but word catalogs.
Juggling was once a synonym for writing.
Somewhere along the way the meaning
of juggling or writing changed.
The library is my laboratory.
It's where I developed my Theory of Silence
—more than a few seconds between sentences is a sin.
I've committed many, at least that's what I've been told.
You could guess who by counting the stains
on my shadow, could guess that the rib God took
was a punch line to His favorite joke.
A woman put the clothes I kept at her apartment
in a hallway in a cardboard box with a note
that said I was only an experiment.
Sacrifice is a science. Science is a side show.
I have a whip and top hat.
I sleep on a glass slide beneath a microscope.
I see the eye in the peephole, studying me closely.

The Scaffolding

1.

When I left home, all I took was a window
knowing there would be times I wanted to look back.
Life is designed to be open, but you knew that.
Still, when people become nosy I draw the curtains.
This is where language stumbles through its destiny
of hiding, privacy, and shame. Though I'm past all of that.

2.

In each lung, a secret lake, waiting,
where everything I own will spend eternity sinking.
How long can a favorite shirt hold its breath and where will it hold it?

3.

There are other secrets hidden in the kidneys.
All that stuff about the heart
is nonsense, nothing more than a pump
incapable of doing two things at once.
Do you know the similarities between skin and wallpaper?
You can write essays about them—I've done it more than once.

4.

Lovers have used my tongue as a red carpet.
It's been said my elbows glow in the dark,

and on hot, humid days I sweat fireflies.
We all have quirks, but this isn't a contest.

5.

A DNA test concluded I'm the descendant
of a rusted car and a lightning storm.

I Could Have Been an Inventor

I'm writing the history of joy
and will prove it was invented
to shill for pain. A simple demonstration,
you're hanging a photograph
of you and a lover; joy.
Nail held to a wall by two fingers.
Hammer in the other hand, pain.
Yes, hypothetical, and simple.
Reality is more complicated.

A woman asked me to swallow a compass
so I would always find my way back to her.
At one time or another,
we're all someone's sandcastle.
My three favorite things about her:
One, she tattooed my Greek name
on her chest just below the neckline.
Two, she wrote nursery rhymes about me.
Three, she ran her tongue over her lips
to wet them before kissing me.

Joy was invented by Kallias in 2021 B.C.
He wrote that joy came to him in a dream.
It's now accepted that dreams
are the desperate moans of the past.
Nothing is known about Kallias' life before joy,
where much of life is lived.
She promised to list three things she liked about me.
She was a disgrace, but so was I.

These Are the Lyrics

The world hangs from heaven by rusty cables.
This is the explanation for everything.
For three days, the odor of tar melting on roof.
Workers, shouting in a different language,
up and down the ladder all morning.
Gravity, gratitude, grave all begin the same.
But this is about endings like the sentence
when it runs out of breath.
The lifeguard diving through the belly
of the wave returns from the ocean alone.
Rescue is a pejorative word when it comes
at the end of a line. Life expectancy
is the songbird in my chest.
The days are ships that strike out against me.

Geography

Each dark morning, a sailor walks down
the narrow steps between the apartment buildings.
His polished shoes scuff the damp concrete.
A hundred miles from sea, the white hat floats
above his black hair and blue uniform.

If the moon is still in the sky a shadow will follow
across the courtyard and into the street.
On their way to school, children who've never seen
the sailor or the sea will run on top of his footprints.
Men with brooms will later sweep away the sand.

Sonnet of Rohrer and Capps

Sixty-four soldiers jump from an airplane into
a commotion of sky, falling and floating,
measured in green silk. The accident report grew
from the men who impersonate small clouds coating
German valleys—except for the two parachutes
that didn't open, dismissed by misfortunes
—the world spinning and spilling beneath their boots.
Now it's urgent that someone build the strong coffins,
and the others, please, stay here to drink and lampoon,
nervously. Yes, we still dispute the time of day.
Some remember morning, others late afternoon.
Some want to know their dead names again, kneel and pray
for a way to not fall. Some say they were clever
to crash into the earth and not fall forever.

Pantoum of the Three Soldiers Killed on the River

When that river's cold water runs through every ugly death
that drags you down where it's darker
—the weight of rifles, thick boots, and helmets, and that last breath!
Three soldiers gone, nothing on the water, not even a marker.

That drags you down where it's darker
when the assault boat sinks and life preservers don't preserve.
Three soldiers gone, nothing on the water, not even a marker.
What do you think as you stand on the bank and observe?

When the assault boat sinks and life preservers don't preserve,
the world changes a little, no judgments here, for better or worse.
What do you think as you stand on the bank and observe?
And what about the three families that will walk behind a hearse?

The world changes a little, no judgments here, for better or worse,
the weight of rifles, thick boots, and helmets, and that last breath!
And what about the three families that will walk behind a hearse
when that river's cold water runs through every ugly death.

THREE

Lost on a Detour

The road is strewn with dead dogs, small black ones that could be hard to see, but the large white ones would be hard to miss; there's also the occasional cat, flat from the neck back. All hit by cars, trucks, perhaps even a yellow motorcycle that struggled to stay upright after striking, then bumping over the body as it hissed its last breath. This carcass-lined road, Braille for some blind god's finger. There's something wrong with the drivers in this town, accident-prone or hateful; and the dogs and cats, stupid or suicidal. When the sun smears the horizon, their shadows stretch and touch in a way they never could when alive, creating the path to glory, one long stain.

The Days of Dead Flies

Marine biologists say flies evolved from shrimp, wings once fins before crawling from the ocean four hundred and thirty million years ago—the first animals to fly. In the last three minutes of their lives, flies are able to travel backwards, their version of a time machine—three minutes into the past. The first flies taught birds formations, the original language; spiders to make webs, the original map. Now, a dozen dead lie on the window sill, two others flap their wings four or five last times. Every day for a week, I find more, no explanation for their sunlit death. Just think how surprised the police were, the purse wrestled from the woman fell to the pavement and a thousand poured out, dead black stars in need of a sky.

A Medical History

The paper clip was invented by Doctor Hélène de La Coste, a surgeon
with the French Army. Its original purpose isn't clear. What is clear
is that Doctor De La Coste designed it as a surgical tool. In a letter
to a cousin, an aide referred to the bent pieces of metal as *le tendon
clop*, suggesting it was meant to hold tendons in place while suturing.
The small clips must have kept slipping from the blood-wet tendons
and were lost inside the arm, leg or whatever gap in the body was
created by battle. Another document suggested the clip was a surgical
probe, bent to curve inside itself for storage purposes. Doctor De
La Coste was killed by British artillery at Waterloo. Along with
other belongings, seven *le tendon clops* were returned to her family
in Toulouse. One *le tendon clop* was used by a young niece on a doll's
hair, no mention of the other six paper clips.

The Cockalorums

I invented the broken pencil. All the old forms of outrage had become passé. My neighbor had already perfected the blank stare. Night after night, I saw him standing in front of a mirror, rehearsing, perfecting, pulling his shoulders back with pride. It was just this sort of behavior that convinced his wife to accept his marriage proposal. If my attempt to patent the broken pencil is unsuccessful there are other inventions to discuss, a dog-shaped cloud drifting out to sea, for instance. The contributions my inventions could add to society would be substantial.

A Welter

We dug the pit, set the spit, then went to the pen to slaughter the pig and found him playing an almost-in-tune piano. I thought the same thing you're thinking, how does he play the black keys? He used an upside-down trough as a bench, played what I thought was "25 Minutes to Go," which, by the way, I never heard on the piano but being a Johnny Cash fan I thought I recognized it. My brother said it sounded more like "My Lord, Closer to Thee." I don't remember the pig actually ever looking at us, but he played faster as we approached. I kicked one foot against the other to knock mud from my shoe. It began to rain, drowning out the music. You know how these things end. We laid planks of wood across the ground as the rain came down harder.

The Arrogance

"If you stand on the beach, reach out and rub the horizon with a pencil eraser, earth and sky become one," Albert Einstein wrote to his sister, Maja; "catastrophic possibilities, I'd rather not consider walking barefoot in the sand." I didn't believe it was possible, but thought there might be something to learn, so I tried. Barefoot on a beach, pants rolled up, arm outstretched, I rubbed an eraser across the horizon. It began to rain. After standing there for a few minutes, I threw my eraser into the sea and drove home thinking of a handmade bullwhip I bought in New Mexico. Instead of the eraser I should have brought the whip to the beach. I believed if I stood in surf and cracked it the whales would know I was there.

Caligula's Mattress

Her mattress was delivered to me the other day. I recognized the blood stain and for an instant thought to wet my finger, drag it over the dried crimson, and see if it would taste like her. The ink stain, from the night I fell asleep writing with an old fountain pen, I recognized that, too, and tried to remember what I was writing. It's been two years since we've slept together on it. I imagine its springs are uneven, making a good sleep unlikely. I imagine this can interrupt a dream. I imagine that she read the magazine article about Caligula that said after having sex he occasionally sent the mattress to the woman. I don't remember if there was an explanation. There are, after all, more important things to remember, like a splinter in the tongue from a wooden chopstick.

The Apprentice Physician Discusses Training

Hands must be disinfected before sharpening needles; warm, not hot water, and Betadine Scrub. The needle is correct once the sting is invisible. Every apprentice learns this the first day. The storm in the chest is incorrectly referred to as heart. This is learned the second day. The nurse, the way she removes a pen from your breast pocket, a noticeable difference between physician and apprentice. Learned the seventh day. Some physicians forget to teach it is unethical to place a stethoscope against a sleeping lover's head and eavesdrop on dreams. Medical school teaches the science of medicine. The apprentice must learn the art, where licentious abandon offers unique satisfaction, think pleasure of mutation, peach into nectarine, for instance. The sugar cube in the pocket, for instance, medical schools say nothing about this yet it brings the necessary luck when a patient's temperature is 109. Nineteen years, the required apprenticeship. On the last day the apprentice learns the sublime cruelty of reaching inside a person to massage a heart, waking the next morning to find blood under the fingernails.

The Apprentice Physician Discusses Transfusion

Every apprentice physician knows the story of the boy laid on Jean-Baptiste Denys' table. Inauguration was invented to lend importance to an event. It's the apprentice physician's charge to memorize the circulation. Blood pooled on the floor. This is how transfusion is taught. A sheep from the neighbor's farm provided the blood. If a physician transfuses to an apprentice, veins splinter. The first transfusion I conducted went awry and a woman closed her eyes. Everything happens after suffering, everything. Yes, as every apprentice physician does, I keep blood in my refrigerator. Don't talk to me about laws. Don't talk to me at all. The boy survived.

FOUR

This Is Another Version of Heroism

for Becky

1.

I was married to a porn star for eight years
though we separated after twenty months.
We never saw each other after that.
This was after the army years and before college.
She taught me that grief and depression
are not the same. She taught me
the heart has an ego. I taught her
that you can be honest and not tell the truth.
To be married to a porn star is difficult at night.
Now let's talk about where the strength
to get out of a bed begins. We had become
battle-blood and dread. In the morning
she was just another young wife
who slept in men's pajamas and said thank you
when coffee and cereal were waiting in the kitchen.
You have two choices in life,
to rise or not rise. It's not as easy as you think.

2.

Her body was an actress, condensation
floating above a river after sunrise, or the river
lying below the condensation, depending
on whether she was the antagonist or protagonist.
Over breakfast she said she was leaving.
I think I replied with a simple "okay,"
though I might have just sobbed.
On our last morning together, she gave me a box

of pencils imprinted with my name.
This was years before I began writing.
Sometimes I pretend she's married again,
we've become friends, and has twin girls
with her freckles thrown in their faces.
Sometime I pretend I'm an unmarked grave
—everything I know about absolution
tells me this is inevitable.
I never used the pencils until today
when I sharpened all of them down to nubs.
She would be flattered by this;
everything was a compliment to her,
even my name, a pile of shavings in a silver cup.

I've Dedicated My Life to My Nightmares

Eat a pomegranate before sleep and you'll dream of suicide,
which this night ended with her reaching for the Smith & Wesson.
A nightmare for her, dream for me. In my version of the dream
she lay on top of me, stuck her tongue in my ear.
Then she sat up into a shaft of moonlight
that glowed on her breasts like two white moons.
There's a theme here, she said. No there's not,
I said. I am a nightmare expert.
Nightmares are not coincidences; this is the one thing we agreed on.
Eating before sleep triggers nightmares that take place at sea.
We covered the pomegranate already.
Listening to music while asleep prevents nightmares.
A girl played a harp at the foot of Pharaoh Sedjefakare's bed
as he slept. He never had a nightmare.

Nightmares for the dead are dreams of life.
Not remembering dreaming is dreaming of being dead.
Men have more nightmares than women, she said,
and then got out of bed looking for food.
She was my therapist, and the truth is we did have sex.
Having sex with your therapist is not uncommon.
That night I found myself clinging to a life preserver
in the middle of the ocean. That's also not uncommon.
When I wake after a nightmare I take a crayon
from under my pillow and change the number on the wall.
My therapist believes I study nightmares to prove my courage.
But that's not true. Only in nightmares is the imagination truly an
    artist.
They are the most vivid dreams, i.e.,
moonlight glowing on her breasts like moons.

Through Purgatory

My severed left hand lies on a lawn
in front of a yellow house.
Smoke floats from the chimney.
Someone peeks out between the curtains.
This is heaven. Odd that only my left hand
is in heaven. That must be God peeking.
Odd that God lives in a yellow house.
Hell is just across the street
with its own lawn, its own yellow house.
My severed right hand lies on that lawn.
The devil peeks out between those curtains.
On the street between heaven and hell
carts stacked with corpses, the unclaimed souls,
are pulled by men with gray faces and hollow eyes.
God and the devil occasionally nod. A cart stops,
a corpse is dragged to a lawn,
sometimes only a leg, nose or ear.
Men and women in various states
of decomposition walk with me.
A woman hugs a frying pan as if it were a baby.
The man carrying a wooden ladder
is looking for the up and down.
The sky has no color, no light or dark.
I walk behind a cart hoping this is only a dream.
As a man pulls a corpse over his shoulder
he tells me everyone hopes that same thing.

The Premonitory

God is a rooster, heaven a barnyard.
Let's take turns being priests,
run our fingers through mud, draw
dirt crosses on our foreheads.
When the world ends
the only thing left will be a hole in the sky.
The last people will sprout wings and fly through it.
Sorrow is the new joy
and living more heroic than dying.
To prepare for this I've changed
my name to Nero and bought a violin.
I want to be good at something;
for now, this will do.
The warm breeze you feel
is the future's hot breath.

This Is the Ticking of a Stopwatch

I had a girlfriend who hypnotized herself
brushing her teeth as she stared in a mirror.
She gave me a list to read
as she stood in a trance, toothpaste dripping
from her chin onto her bathrobe or T-shirt,
depending how cold the morning.
I stuck to the script, for the most part.
Later, when she burnt toast then was ticketed
for not paying a parking meter,
she complained that I ordered her to do it.
But I didn't, I told her other things.
You would have, too, given the chance.
After sex she had me squeeze her lungs,
expelling what remained of my breath.
I told her I dreamed I was a bat
flying panicked across the bedroom.
She told me it wasn't a dream, pointed
to small scuff marks on the ceiling as proof.
For the longest time, I was the child
crawling from the ocean,
a smoke signal disassembled by wind
—she was everything else.
The clock's hands stopped and so did we.
Like everyone else, we were being timed.

Ooh La La

Looking back, I now believe it was the train whistle in the dark
that triggered her orgasms and not me. But we were in love.

We lived on an island in the middle of a lake. She said my heart was a suspension
bridge that linked our souls together, or some such rot. I wanted to
believe her.

The only thing she ever gave me was a choice. I could be an
amusement park, alarm clock,
or a crowd watching us at night. I never chose. The expectations were
never clear.

Then we learned the limitations and seldom talked to each other,
though the love-making continued each night.

Once, she pushed me into a coffin and put her hand inside my pants.
Need, not lust, was our lingua franca. She feigned surprise in French.

Our last time together was an attempt at genius invention,
dissolving into a maelstrom . . . we christened it Survival Training.

Time is skillful with a sleight of hand called memory.
Every few years I consider sending her a card.

The truth is . . . we weren't a relationship, we were a destination.
You could have found us on a map.

Pity, Sublime and Punctual, Arrives

The second time we got together
she was magic. I was a gimmick.
I'm being hard on myself.
I'll start over. The second time
we got together she was what I wasn't.
We were learning the importance of a buoy
when a dorsal fin rises between whitecaps,
the importance of a pillow
between sleep and a pistol.

The waiter brought my salad and her soup.
Charming sounds of silverware against china.
As we walked to the car, night choked on darkness
and our hands inside leather gloves turned
to ashes, our lips and tongues to smoke.

The Sainthood

When I learned I was on the Vatican's shortlist for sainthood
I went to the store to try on halos, and that night, sleep
riveted darkness to my eyes so black no sin
could penetrate. My lover was troubled
by the prospect. Would she be required to pray naked
on her knees to me? We had often prayed
beside the bed; sometimes I cheated, opening my eyes
to see her wine-glass shaped breasts resting on the blanket.
For me, the sex that followed was sublime.
I was sure God was rewarding me.
She was bothered that I was the one blessed
by potential sainthood. She didn't enjoy
the sex, which in her mind made her a better candidate.
She became depressed and angry, lost confidence in her faith,
though she attempted to keep this to herself.
We spent mornings waiting at the mailbox
for the letter from the Vatican.
When it didn't arrive we went back inside,
she put on her shortest robe and made breakfast.
I sat at the kitchen table, stared down at fried eggs
on burnt toast while she hid behind the newspaper
doing the crossword puzzle, sipping coffee and asked
if I knew an eleven-letter word for smug that starts with e?
One morning the mailman came walking up the driveway
singing *still all my song shall be, nearer, my God, to Thee.*
As he reached in his bag he was struck by a bolt of lightning.
I ran for the fire extinguisher. She called 911.
The ambulance took him, and the mailbag
and its letters, cinders and ashes ascending.

Dating Advice from the Bible

I descended heaven on the back of a donkey,
my stomach lined with rusted chains,
links the size of a cow's eye. These are things
women find attractive about me.
The truth is these are things
I say before asking a woman out.
It's no coincidence I told a woman
who ordered me on my hands and knees
that love appears in the Bible 302 times.
I told the woman who loved dogs
that mine keeps a pistol in his doghouse.
When he wags his tail you'll glimpse it.
I told her I'm happy when I play jazz on the spoons.
I told her God knows nothing about romance.
Told her religion was invented to sanctify subservience.
Read the Bible closely. You'll learn
angels fall with their wings on fire,
the ringing in your ears is God whispering, and a woman
putting her tongue in a man's mouth is a display of ownership.
If the Bible is a utensil, what does that say about us?
Pretend that isn't a question.
Pretend you share a soul with a stranger,
it's been known to happen.
Pretend you weep at the sound
of a butter knife falling,
just pretend, it's not difficult.

Lothario and Dulcinea

Hammerheads are the only sharks that cry.
Biology? Or are hammerheads the only sensitive sharks?
Humans didn't cry, science says,
until about 250,000 years ago.
Crying was a complex form of communication
for Neanderthals. I, like you, share
four percent of my DNA with them.
and also use crying as Neanderthals did.
I told this to a woman in a motel room
as I undressed. Crying is learned
like a magician learns to hide a playing card
behind his fingers, Jack of Clubs,
for instance. Crying is learned like a woman
learns burlesque dancing.

She spun around, bent back at the waist,
put a red silk over the lamp shade.
That's why the lady is a tramp, Sinatra sang.
Motel rooms are dilemmas.
The room turned red. She said that,
like the Neanderthal, she never had sex
with a man she didn't first bite to the point of blood.
What could make a shark cry?
Time is an assembly line.
Pants folded over the back of a chair.
God banging on the door.
Towel wrapped around my hand.
I'm an acceptable substitute
for a god. It almost hurts.

The Performance

I bought a wedding cake in a pawnshop,
a single layer of yellow frosting,
the bride on top was a head taller than the groom.
I sold it for a small profit at the courthouse
across the street to a teenage couple,
the bride with a baby bump. They shared
the cake with the others waiting for a wedding license,
paying traffic tickets, and a handcuffed man
standing between two police officers in front of an elevator.
I used the money to buy a hot dog from a cart on the sidewalk.
I didn't mind when it began to rain—the coolness
of a dampening shirt, water flattening
my hair, heat lifting from my skin.
The rain grew heavy, darkening the sky,
washing away the shadows. The rolls
of thunder in the distance could have been mistaken
for applause or artillery, depending where you grew up.
Though one often follows the other.

I Once Changed for You

Now that my world is made of paper I look
into an endless sheet of white when I drag
the razor's edge across the stubble on my chin
and turn a paper faucet for chaff.
I am a theory, no, an experiment.
It was too difficult being a sacred lost and found.
It was too difficult being a stone man living
in a stone world, comings and goings announced by stone shoes.
Did I feel more comfortable in your arms
when I was a night sky and could spit
the wind back into the trees?
I don't know where my eyes end and the world begins.
I don't know what I'll be next.
I would return your love but I forgot where I put it.
No, I don't know what I'll be next, but guesses can be made.
Taking the long way to a grave,
each of us is a funeral procession of one.

This, Too, Is a Love Poem

Freeze if you're caught in the open
when an illumination shell explodes
above, nothing catches enemy eyes
like quick movements. Your heart
becomes a firebox in a steam engine;
your lungs, the boiler; but the foliage
on your uniform turns you into the landscape
as that man-made sun floats beneath its silk to earth.
There are as many ways to say this as reasons why.
I will title this memory with the outline
of your face and damp grass waiting
to be flattened by our bodies,
a thousand beautiful cruelties
with a fork stuck in them and our echoes
rising into a statue after we're gone.

The Funerary

She made paintbrushes from her mother's hair
and one year after the funeral painted
a watercolor portrait of the kitchen.
Yellow morning light through the window
because it was often morning.
Though her mother was always in the kitchen
she was not in the painting, only her shadow was.
This is what death does. On the table, not coffee but a cup.
She painted the light green walls
and the suggestion of two chairs.
She painted the basement door slightly ajar,
darkness seeping from the sides.

What comes up from a basement decides many things
for a daughter without her mother.
The daughter sits in her mother's chair.
The daughter sips her coffee by the window.
The daughter imagines her mother wandering
among the trees of the backyard or haunting
the portrait in which she does not appear.
Instead of a frame, she put the portrait
in a pine box and buried it.

The Terrene

I was a human mailbox, stood at the end
of a wealthy woman's driveway, waiting
for letters and packages civil servants
or private firms were obligated to deliver.
According to the census I am not the only person
who lists "mailbox" as their occupation.
In the early morning, worms crawled from the wet grass
to warm themselves on the pavement. I gave them names
though this is something I kept to myself until now.
At the end of the day I placed the mail on an ornate table
she bought in Verona. Once, wearing only a green bathrobe,
she stood at the end of the hallway sipping bourbon,
told me to open the phone bill and read out loud
the thirty-two numbers she was charged for calling.
She turned, pressed her back flat against the wall
and closed her eyes. I thought she was listening
for a particular number but when I finished
she returned to her bedroom without a word.
In the nineteen years I worked for her
she wrote only one letter. She's been dead for eleven years
but it would still be a betrayal to say to whom she wrote.
Stillness was one of the job's pleasures.
"Postage" in an ancient language
can be translated to mean threat,
something I only understood after she died.

Come All Ye Faithful

Waiting for a flight at the airport a woman glanced at me,
then stared. It's been years but occasionally it still happens.
There was a time I was famous. My book, *The History
of Medieval Northern European Dentistry,*
was an international bestseller in the dental history category.
You can't write a book like mine without research.
A private collector in Australia keeps Adolph Hitler's bicuspids in a
    safe.
Three of Joan of Arc's teeth belong to the Vatican.
My wisdom teeth are on display at the British Dental Association
    Museum.
The earliest dentist known by name is Hesi-re. He practiced in Egypt,
five thousand years ago, little else is known about him.

The history of the mouth is the history of everything ever said.
Scientists once believed language originates
in the left hemispheric cortex of the brain.
This theory developed while studying silence that followed
being struck on the head with a large piece of wood.
We now know that language exists in the tongue,
the hyoglossus, to be exact, a tongue muscle. This is why
the Latin word for "language," *lingua,*
is also the Latin word for hyoglossus.
The Latin word for "guard," *praesidio,* is also Latin for "teeth."
You know where this is going: language, puzzle, teeth, clues.

In Germany it was common to kiss a donkey to relieve toothaches.
In Japan a groom gave his bride a tooth on their first anniversary.
In Jamaica a tooth plays a central role in three deadly voodoo curses.
When I'm lonely, really lonely, I bite myself.
So did Mae West, Thomas Jefferson, and Margaret Thatcher.
Closing the eyes in concert with the bite

distinguishes this from sophomoric theatrics.
A mouth is an anthology. Teeth are stories.
No two people have an identical story.
The most decadent thing I did with royalties from the book:
paid a beautiful woman to follow me and retie my shoelaces when
　　they loosened.

I'm vain enough to believe I still resemble my author photograph.
I believe the row of bite marks on my forearm resembles the
　　Hawaiian Islands.
Still, there's more to believe. Inside everyone, someone famous
is waiting to die, *herkos odonton,* allowing his soul
to escape the barrier of his teeth.
The woman staring at me wore a loose, white blouse
and black slacks that would have showed off her figure if she stood.
I was hoping she would ask for my autograph.
I wouldn't have asked for anything in return.
But I could picture her bite mark on my thigh.
Everyone has done this at least once, but this isn't about you.

The Supermundane

I've been hiding for a long time,
at least that's how I explain my loneliness to myself.
I often change my name, occupation, too. Last year
I was employed making extra-thick shoelaces,
popular with suicides; the year before that,
pretended to have important credentials.
I can prove that the past is geography.
Though I'm undecided if the future
is a game of darts. My favorite occupation
was observer, and not just because I was good at it.
How many occupational hazards can you name?
My favorite is the shadow the large hand leaves
on the face as time passes and passes.
If you put a stethoscope to my chest
what would you hear? Hint,
it's been raining inside me for years.

The Bad Years

He tossed a pebble in a pond, beginning
the slow expanding rippling circles that never stopped.
It was the quietest thing in the world. Some say, even quieter than
    death.
Some say, this caused the bad years that would continue until the
    ripples stopped.
Some say, the only way they would stop is to retrieve the pebble.

One night he stood beside the pond and watched
the water rippling in the moonlight.
He remembered someone telling him
the pond is eight feet deep.
He removed his shirt and hoped
his fingers would remember the pebble.

There Are Always Decisions

We waded naked into a river, the cold
water was startling. I wanted to stop
but her taunting was effective. I told her
I wasn't a man of rivers, told her
rivers were like changing stories
that could only be understood
while we sleep, with images only possible in dreams.
I remember water slapping my face,
goose bumps on her breasts, the river tangled
in her black hair, and the pale green walls
of a motel that didn't provide towels.
We dried ourselves with the sheets.
Religious scholars still argue
whether God invented death or discovered
it in the failures He left in us. For an instant,
she died in that room, and was brought back
with electrical jolts. The past can ruin any image
lasting longer than an instant. The ambulance's
red light took the bottom of the window
like a sunset takes the bottom of a sky.
Today the important parts of this story
are the darkening blue sky that was hard to the touch,
the toast and cottage cheese she ate in the morning
as I dropped coins in the pay phone.
Someone told me she's now a dentist in a small town.
Someone else told me she married a soldier
and was killed in an auto accident in Italy.
I haven't decided which story I want to believe.

This Is Where I Stop Apologizing

I am a lost and found.
I have toy soldiers that belonged to her dead brother,
sex toys that have been in my underwear drawer
for years; yes, and other things
that could make people blush; yes,
the nuts and bolts of one life or another.
I am an assembly line of misdemeanors.
Seven unopened envelopes, rubber-banded together,
below the kitchen sink next to the garbage disposal motor.
The oldest envelope references a police car's
passenger window smashed with a bourbon bottle.
In two cultures I am a pictograph
for the holiest love or something equally wonderful.
In three cultures I am a pictograph
for a sobbing boy in the arms of his father.
In another culture I am a pictograph
for a damp wall; imagine that, me, a damp wall.
My body is a dictionary for words
that only exist in Greek tragedies.
Finally, I am unapologetic in every culture.
That alone should have been enough
to make me part of her vocabulary.
We disagreed, she and I. One of us spoke
about the privileges of being lost.
The other spoke fondly of being found.
I'll leave you to decide who said what.
But at the risk of appearing self-serving,
the first line of my résumé states,
I am not just the residue of miracles.
It was my hard work and skills
that kept our lungs panting in cadence.

Science

for Lara

I told her a swarm of bees flying from my mouth
doesn't make me a monster.
She told me being mistaken for a prostitute is résumé-worthy.
My tongue, I said, was a formidable weapon,
but not in the way you think. Her next confession
was that ice had formed on her learning curve.
Once past the small talk, we traded blood-stained hearts.
Then came that dream, a raccoon was sitting next to me on a bus
and showing me photographs of her that he carried in his wallet.
That makes no sense, she said, raccoons don't carry wallets.
Interesting that she didn't mention the bus.
We had yet to decide which causes deserved our sympathy,
everything from flying monkey rescue
to clean water in Uganda was on the table.
But now I'm getting off the subject.
We made love in a lightning orchard.
We pretended we were in hiding and slept in the closet.
She drew a map on the bottom of my feet, in case I got lost.
Yes, being broken is heroic and glorious.

We

For firewood, we disassembled a house.
For food, we consulted the weeds and the slaughtered goat.
For religion, we said a constellation was a man pointing to a heaven.
For love, we closed our eyes and feigned ignorance.
We did other things, too, but there's just so much
we wanted to be remembered for.
The warehouses were full
and our feet were thick with blisters.
There was nowhere else to carry our stories.

Judgment Days

1.

The men with smoke-stained faces, their thick yellow jackets
finally open, drive away; and I stand in the charred remains
of my living room. The sofa, flattened black ash.
A wall erased in smoky smudge. Three thousand books,
ashen hulks. Strange, how one chair still has legs.
I can't understand flames, their choices,
or better said, their tastes. One bedroom untouched.
Picking through blackened possessions, cursing, stopping
to write something about embers, a code for loss.

2.

Each time someone lingers on these chiaroscuro words
the wooden floor begins to spark.
The television explodes. The sirens
will again arrive before the trucks.
The bookcases will be licked red and black.
A wall falls. Again, the water. The damp hoses,
rolled and returned to the fire trucks.
Men with smoke-stained faces, their thick yellow jackets open,
drive away; and I stand in the charred remains.
These nights have names—Wolf, Pig Stain, Breath Waiting
—when I try to speak, my tongue is like drying cement.

3.

Once the trucks are tucked behind sliding doors
and someone begins to read, the spit and spark
of the fire starts over. Even sins
need practice before they're perfect.
The same men return to the same house,
where they'll jump from their trucks
to which they'll later return when the damp hoses
are rolled, and picks and axes with pieces of
my home stowed for the journey
to the station where the klaxon breaks men from their sleep.

4.

Someone's nightmare wants companionship.
Someone brought this on himself.
Smoke scrapes stars from the sky.
I stand on the lawn shouting as if the fire has ears.

Night Comes Home After the Business of Darkness

In the back of the taxi, we carried on
like the driver couldn't see.
When I stood in that light rain
to pay, the driver gestured at my fly.
Later in the hotel, I pretended
not to notice her sitting on the bed
as I made a bow tie at the mirror.
Women in corridors wore black gowns.
The elevator ride was uneventful,
though someone commented
on the pleasant chimes each time it stopped.
How many bar drinks can you name
that contain the word blood?
My eyelids are doors.
I miss the sound of us kissing.
I didn't have an answer when she asked
how long we have to be together
before we start telling the truth.

We're All Famous in a Mysterious Sort of Way

It's Christmas Eve, the rasp of clearing
my throat sounds like a storm in the distance.
More people die on December twenty-fifth
than any other day of the year.
I'm convinced that ropes and pulleys
hold up the trees and skeletons
of clouds drift in the sky above.
In the seventeen years I've lived
in this house eleven squirrels have died in the yard
—all of which I've used a stick to push
onto cardboard and carry to the trash,
strange what we become good at.
I'm the eighteenth person who has written
out the entire King James Bible in longhand
on yellow legal pads. It was a contest.
I came in second. I've yet to decide
what I want to be remembered for.
I'm convinced we're God's favorite magic trick.
Do you remember the teeth of His holy saw
against your belly as He began
to cut you in half again and again?

The History of All This

We all have secrets. You, me, all of us,
we're nothing more than machines, of sorts.
When a woman looks into my eyes
she sees pieces of herself reflected
from the small mirrors that were surgically implanted
beneath my irises. Standing on a crowded bus,
I once noticed smoke drifting from the ears
of the man in front of me.
I tapped him on the shoulder and told him.
He nodded politely, said thank you.
Some things you probably don't know,
people born with only nine fingers score higher on IQ tests
and hell averages eleven inches of rain annually.
Yes, I find solace in facts. There have been times
I've forgotten who and what I love.
So I sit at the kitchen table and make lists.
Last night I dreamed of my name.
This might be my first real attempt at sincerity.
This morning birds with leather wings filled the sky.

Like Many Other Technologies, My Dreams Are Now Obsolete

A woman poured honey on my thighs
then licked it off. This was the closest we came
to love. A more honest version would have involved
feeding each other to the lions.
This isn't to say we were pagans. This is to say
when I whistled I expected something to happen.
She preferred something to happen when she stood,
though that was confusing, like in the restaurant
when she pushed her chair away from the table,
stood up to go the restroom. I could say more
but truth swells in my throat, think chicken bone.
This is to say love requires more than a thimble
of cruelty. What would you have done?
For most narratives, a self-induced trance
is preferable to feigning epilepsy.
Relationships are stories
two people write at the same time.
We were a bowl of bruised apples.
Great sentences are metaphors for snakes,
shaping themselves for comfort after devouring
something larger than themselves.
I stored my sins in a warehouse, I still do.
It has a large door with a faded orange juice
advertisement. Her only sin, me, required no storage.
She never said why she cut my silk ties in half.
I never asked. I never said goodbye.
I put a storm on a leash and walked home.
Imagine the rain parting as I go.

How to Tell a Story, but Not Why

I'm not sure if I'm afraid or embarrassed to say
my mother is rehearsing her death. She lies in bed
holding her breath, lets the casual observer believe she's gone.
But there's nothing casual here and my brother and I don't want to
     practice
the roles she's laid out for us. I can only imagine
those fierce tribes that fashioned arrowheads
from the bones of grizzly bears. I'm trying to be fierce, trying
to find a grizzly bear as the future circles my bed
—the priests with smoking pots of incense swaying from chains.
They should be circling her bed
but dead and dread are too close to call
—someone else has to explain the difference.

There's no logic to this world; in the end,
it's an origami Icarus falling from a sky,
in the end the word orphan becomes a verb.
The fierceness required to get out of bed each morning.
One day I'm going to stop being afraid, I swear,
but for now, I'm continuing. I'm not the first person
to dress up death and pretend
a cemetery is a good place for a picnic.

If you asked my mother about this
she would deny it, all of it.
The fierceness of her lies.
The ferocity of Icarus falling. Just before you die,
an instant or two at most, your shadow
disappears, then everything follows.
My mother will never read a word of this.
It's not her story.

The Orison

After hours behind the delicatessen counter
—slicing meat, building sandwiches
—my father comes home from work.
His white shirt, name embroidered
above the pocket, is stained.
These were the days we wrote phone numbers
in pencil on the kitchen wall beside the phone.
Nightmares are technical schools a woman told me.
Later that night a possum crawled through the pet door.
The commotion woke us. The glow of moonlight
on the possum's long white snout, her parrot
lifeless in its mouth. My father stands
at the kitchen sink, rolls up his sleeves,
splashes cold water on his face, runs
wet hands through his thick black hair.
There are degrees of death; talking to a ghost
is first, then premonition, even déjà vu.
Hierarchy is a personal matter.

The morning before my father died,
my mother found him on the bed,
pressing a pillow into the mattress,
sobbing and saying he was suffocating his shadow.
I'm too close to this story to tell it objectively.
My high school biology teacher stood in front
of the class and crushed a baby rabbit's throat,
only took half a minute, legs kicking
as it hung from his hand. Mortality
isn't the opportunity you think it is.

The woman put her parrot in a jewelry box,
buried it in the yard. It won't be long

before this is a bunch of ballyhoo
and I come clean with my regrets.
My father's last day is in a hospital room.
An old black and white movie
flickering through static on a television,
my mother's shadow on the wall.

We Were the Great Admirers of the Many Fears

This was the night of the scar-pocked sky, the night
gravediggers pledged to dig three holes each day
for as long as necessary. And then a hundred men drowned.
The ocean no longer found a need to exaggerate.
Its giant shadow resembled a sinking ship.
The mountains in the distance were on fire.
The lovers would have to find new places to rendezvous.
At the end of the day, we opened umbrellas
to keep the ashes off our shoulders
and walked home resembling a colony of red ants.
This is how a line drawn on butcher paper
becomes a dangerous threshold to cross.
We were experienced, knew how
to find new things to be afraid of,
even the most ordinary future is relentless.
Sooner or later, we would be tired again
and forever; and then that, too, would end.

Somewhere Along the Learning Curve

I was the heart of a spider attacking a fly.
I was at sea, a lifeboat without survivors.
Ants crawling along my finger caused me to sob.
For years, I believed these facts compelled her to love me.
Now I know better. I was her favorite riddle
that she stopped trying to solve. Soon
we pantomimed lovemaking and our moans
hissed and stuttered like a choking engine.
When she said I was her Sisyphus, I replied,
"Wait a minute, I said that about you first."

A man has to know when to call it quits.
Going forward, I'll attempt excuses before apologies.
It doesn't matter which of us said I love you first
or who changed their mind. These things happen.
The point is I have copious notes to study
from our years together. I'll only forget
the first rule of fire-eating once,
to slowly and steadily exhale
before closing my lips around the flame.

The Gathering

I'm scheduled to have my tongue set afire, not because I said
everything wrong. I said everything right. I told you,
for instance, that the moon is closer tonight. Stare at the chalk-white
    plate
of its face, you can almost see the two golf balls, five flags,
twelve pairs of boots, ninety-six bags of human waste,
and twelve Hasselblad cameras that were left there.

Light is nothing more than the absence of darkness.
My soul is nothing more than God's stale breath, and so is yours.
The more accusatory the language, the more beautiful.
The moon is closer tonight. I have seven different space suits in my
    closet;
for different occasions, not for different days of the week.
Yes, I am a bit of a scientist, also a bit of a prophet, perhaps more so.
On three occasions I've been mistaken for a preposterous religion,
on another occasion a not so preposterous religion.
Only modesty compels me to use the word "mistaken."

The last woman who put her hand in mine was asking for something.
She saw my nose and lips widen when I pressed them against the
    window,
an image some cultures believe foreshadows something like frogs falling
from the sky which I don't believe at all. But the truth is, proverbs
    predicted me
and that feels like being pushed down a flight of stairs and left splayed
on the floor while people stare and whisper, "he had no say in his
    achievements."

I'm scheduled to be the replacement for the target's bullseye,
not as punishment for my veracity, but a sweet recompense
for the steadfast belief that if I loved myself more

this would echo like a clean-water creek, instead
it sounds like a knife tearing a screen door.
Though I do love myself more today than seventeen years ago,
resignation not progress. The moon is closer tonight and fear
prompts people to pray. Seventeen percent of Americans believe
God lives on the moon. One day they'll say it was me all along
who was God's one good ear. One day they'll say
that—from start to finish—I was a choir. One day every woman who
    ever believed me
will be sainted and part of the fresco I'm painting on the mansion walls.
Every woman who ever doubted me will also be sainted
and part of the fresco I'm painting.
Every man who refuses to make this his own will join me
on my knees barking with the dogs
and those who do will grow wings.

Acknowledgments

Grateful acknowledgment is made to the editors of the following publications in which these works or earlier versions of them previously appeared:

Agni: "My Father Is Still Dead";
Another Chicago Magazine: "The Orison";
The Antioch Review: "Night Comes Home After the Business of Darkness";
Carrier Pigeon: "The Juggernaut," "Prognosis," and "I Carry a Moth in a Pillbox with Me Everywhere";
Conduit: "The Bad Years";
Cultural Weekly: "Like Many Other Technologies, My Dreams Are Now Obsolete" and "Let's Become a Ghost Story";
Diagram: "Pity, Sublime and Punctual, Arrives";
Field: "The Scaffolding" and "I Could Have Been an Inventor";
Five Points: "Perfecting the Dog Paddle";
Fixional: "The Cockalorums," "A Welter," and "Caligula's Mattress";
The Florida Review: "Sooner or Later, Everything Comes Out";
Gettysburg Review: "Come All Ye Faithful";
Hotel Amerika: "Lost on a Detour" and "The Days of Dead Flies";
The Laurel Review: "Drama of a Sigh";
Nimrod International Journal: "Ex Cathedra";
Pratik: "This Is Another Version of Heroism," "Somewhere Along the Learning Curve," and "Let's Become a Ghost Story";
Smartish Pace: "Through Purgatory" and "Premonitory";
The Southern Review: "We";
Wait a Minute, I Have to Take Off My Bra: "The Hardness."

Thanks for reading and commenting on the poems, and cheerleading along the way: Ian Randall Wilson, Alexis Orgera, William Burnside, Becky Fink, Meg Kearney, Nin Andrews, George Higgins, Paula Yoo, Elise Martin, Shivani Mehta, Leslie Blanco, Megan Pinto, Jeff

Friedman, Marion Boyer, Karen Schubert, Kathi McGookey, Sammy Greenspan, Rosalynde Vas, Lynne Aline, Martin Ott, Jay Brecker, Tony Barnstone, Peter Serchuk, Judy French, Susan Hayden, Laura Kasischke, Harold Watson, Patrick Ballogg, and Peter Conners for his continuing faith in my poems.

About the Author

Originally from New York City, Rick Bursky now lives in Los Angeles. He teaches copywriting at USC's Annenberg School of Communications and occasionally teaches poetry for UCLA Extension Writers' Program. His previous full-length collections are *I'm No Longer Troubled by the Extravagance* (BOA Editions, 2015), *Death Obscura* (Sarabande Books, 2010), and *The Soup of Something Missing* (Bear Star Press, 2004). His chapbook, *The Invention of Fiction*, was published by Hollyridge Press in 2005. He has a BFA from Art Center College of Design in Pasadena and an MFA from Warren Wilson College.

BOA Editions, Ltd.
American Poets Continuum Series

Colophon

BOA Editions, Ltd., a not-for-profit publisher of poetry and other literary works, fosters readership and appreciation of contemporary literature. By identifying, cultivating, and publishing both new and established poets and selecting authors of unique literary talent, BOA brings high-quality literature to the public. Support for this effort comes from the sale of its publications, grant funding, and private donations.

The publication of this book is made possible, in part, by the special support of the following individuals:

Anonymous
James Long Hale
Joe McElveney
Boo Poulin
Steven O. Russell & Phyllis Rifkin-Russell
David W. Ryon
Robert Thomas
William Waddell & Linda Rubel